THE OLYMPIANS' GUIDE TO WINNING THE GAME OF LIFE

< COMPILED BY BUD GREENSPAN >

Publisher: W. Quay Hays
Editorial Director: Peter Hoffman
Editor: Amy Spitalnick
Art Director: Chitra Sekhar
Production Director: Trudihope Schlomowitz

For information:
General Publishing Group, Inc.
2701 Ocean Park Boulevard
Santa Monica, CA 90405

Library of Congress Cataloging-in-Publication Data
The Olympians' guide to winning the game of life / compiled by Bud
Greenspan.
    p.   cm.
    ISBN 1-57544-060-1
    1. Athletes-Quotations. 2. Olympics. 3. Success. 4. Athletes-Conduct
of life. I.Greenspan, Bud.
GV706.55.O59   1997
796.02-dc21   97-16423
                      CIP

Printed in the USA
by RR Donnelley & Sons Company
10 9 8 7 6 5 4 3 2 1

General Publishing Group
Los Angeles

It is dawn...the early morning fog has not yet lifted. Before the sun breaks the horizon...hundreds of athletes throughout the world begin their day...as they have in the past...as they will continue to do in the future. This ritual is repeated everyday...on the beaches...the countryside...the mountains...gymnasiums...swimming pools...tracks....The already great and those who aspire to be...share the same dream...the pursuit of excellence.

—*Bud Greenspan*

DEDICATION

To Nancy Beffa, who for a quarter of a century reached for the stars so that I could grab hold of some of them.

SPECIAL THANKS

To Suzanne Beffa, whose persistence and dedication made this book a reality.

To Sydney Thayer and Ted Batenburg, whose contributions were invaluable.

TABLE OF CONTENTS

THE OLYMPIANS' GUIDE TO

*C*itius, *altius, fortius*...swifter, higher, stronger.

—*Olympic motto*

CAMARADERIE

any athletes compete in the Olympics to bring honor to their country. But, more important, they should appreciate the Olympic spirit: the spirit of an international community of friendship, a spirit of friendship in the midst of a struggle for human improvement.

—Raul Gonzalez, Mexico
track: 1 gold, 1 silver, 1984 Los Angeles

There was the feeling of helping to bridge the gap between the old and new—the indefinable poetic charm of knowing one's self thus linked with the past, a successor to the great heroic figures of olden times...

—Ellery Clark Sr., United States
track and field: 2 gold, 1896 Athens
(on competing in the first Olympic
Games of the modern era)

We came there as individuals, and yet we left with a bond, a shared experience that has defined all of our lives and that can never, ever change. We did it together. I went on to win an individual medal on the parallel bars—which was great but has no meaning to me compared to that team thing, because, to me, that's what it's all about.

—Bart Conner, United States
gymnastics: 2 gold, 1984 Los Angeles

11

My favorite gold medal? That's an easy question. It was the relay, because I won that with my Tennessee State Tigerbelle teammates, and we could celebrate together.

—*Wilma Rudolph, United States*

track: 3 gold, 1960 Rome

*T*he hope is that our athletes can go abroad and extend the hand of friendship to the young people of other countries. They will return to their communities and businesses with that experience, so when they become leaders they will remember these Olympic ideals. People will preserve the peace of the world. Not governments. People.

—*Jack Shea, United States*
speed skating: 2 gold, 1932 Lake Placid

*B*y your sportsmanship, self-sacrifice and courage, you embody all that is right with the Olympic ideal.

—*I.O.C. President Juan Antonio Samaranch*
(upon presenting Canada's Lawrence Lemieux with a special award for saving his competitors from near drowning during the yachting competition at the 1988 Seoul Games)

*W*e have shown everyone that sportsmanship is something which binds peoples of the world. It is something which creates peace. And our relationship sets an example.

—Valerios Leonidis, Greece
weightlifting: 1 silver, 1996 Atlanta (on his relationship with Turkish weightlifter Naim Suleymanoglu; the two each set world records in head-to-head competition at the Atlanta Games and are good friends despite a history of tense relations between their countries)

*E*mil stands up and takes off his little cap. He comes to attention as if he's saluting me, and he kisses me and says, "I am glad for you, my dear friend." To me, this is worth all the gold in the world. For if Zatopek had not existed, being an Olympic champion would have meant nothing for me. But with Zatopek... it is the destiny that was written for me.

—*Alain Mimoun, France*
track: 1 silver, 1948 London; 2 silver, 1952 Helsinki; 1 gold, 1956 Melbourne (on the moments after finally defeating friend and adversary Emil Zatopek of Czechoslovakia; he had finished second to Zatopek in three previous Olympic races)

*I*t didn't matter to me whether I won or lost. I took pleasure in competing and meeting with other competitors. That was the most important thing...

—Birger Ruud, Norway
ski jumping: 1 gold, 1932 Lake Placid; 1 gold, 1936
Garmisch-Partenkirchen; 1 silver, 1948 St. Moritz

*I*n the Olympics there is a sense of tremendous camaraderie with your competitors. It is part of what I like to call the shared energy of competition. You're not competing against your comrades, you're participating with them.

—*Andrea Mead-Lawrence, United States*
alpine skiing: 2 gold, 1952 Oslo

*T*he battle for second between [Sueo] Oe and me in Berlin continued into the evening until there wasn't enough light to see. We woke up the next morning and were shocked that I had been ranked second and Oe third, though we had each cleared the same height. We felt we gave an equal effort, so we had our medals cut in half and resoldered. Then we each had one that was half silver and half bronze. These became known as the Medals of Eternal Friendship.

—*Shuhei Nishida, Japan*
pole vault: 1 silver, 1932 Los Angeles;
1 silver, 1936 Berlin

COMPETITION

*H*e [coach Sammy Lee] tried to instill in me and all his divers that it's important to win, but you want to win when your competitors are at their best, not when they're at their worst. And to me, that's sportsmanship.

—*Bobby Webster, United States*
diving: 1 gold, 1960 Rome; 1 gold, 1964 Tokyo

*T*t was hard for me to stand above my mentor on the victory podium. I felt like I had taken away his medal. Then again, he has four gold medals already. Maybe he could spare one.

—Norm Bellingham, United States
kayak: 1 gold, 1988 Seoul (trained with Ian Ferguson of New Zealand, winner of 3 gold medals in the 1984 Los Angeles Games; Ferguson won the silver to Bellingham's gold in Seoul)

21

*A*s far as my competitors are concerned, of course they were important. However, my major opponent was time.

—*Valery Borzov, USSR*
track: 2 gold, 1 silver, 1972 Munich;
2 bronze, 1976 Montreal

I must compete against myself. This is the only way. Sure I compete for my country. Sure I'm French Canadian, and I compete for my province. But first I compete for myself, against myself.

—*Sylvie Bernier, Canada*
diving: 1 gold, 1984 Los Angeles

I had my own tactics and knew my strengths very well. Even when I knew my competitor was weaker than me, I would still let him go ahead. The important thing for me was to go smoothly along the distance. If you don't calculate your strength correctly, you lose much more in the finish than in the start because in the start, everybody's strong.

—Vyacheslav Ivanov, USSR
rowing: 3 gold, 1956 Melbourne,
1960 Rome, 1964 Tokyo

*J*ust run your own race. Don't worry what the others are doing.

—*Joan Benoit, United States*
marathon: 1 gold, 1984 Los Angeles

25

*O*nce I'm in the competition pavilion, I never follow what the other gymnasts are doing. I totally concentrate on what I have to do. I work on my own body. I do everything I can to concentrate on remaining self-assured and confident.

—*Ecaterina Szabo, Romania*
gymnastics: 4 gold, 1 silver, 1984 Los Angeles

f I'm going to compete, I'm going to give everything that I have. Whatever avenue or venture I take, I was always taught: Never say die.

—Bob Hayes, United States
track: 2 gold, 1964 Tokyo

*T*he very first track event I partici-
pated in was a cross-country race,
and I finished 32nd. I vowed never to run
again. However, being a competitive person,
I just couldn't believe that I could be 32nd
in anything.

—*Andy Stanfield, United States*
track: 2 gold, 1952 Helsinki;
1 silver, 1956 Melbourne

I keep two ideas in my mind always: winning a competition gives me confidence for the next one, and having a challenging spirit. I don't like to lose to anybody.

—*Kenji Ogiwara, Japan*
nordic combined: 1 gold, 1992 Albertville;
1 gold, 1994 Lillehammer

I don't mind losing...but I don't like it.

—*Barney Ewell, United States*
track: 1 gold, 2 silver, 1948 London (lost the
100-meter dash in a photo finish)

I always ran through fear—of being beaten. It brought out the best in me, being terrified of being beaten.

—Shirley Strickland, Australia

track: 1 silver, 2 bronze, 1948 London;

1 gold, 1 bronze, 1952 Helsinki;

2 gold, 1956 Melbourne

The stimulus of competition is much greater than anything else I can possibly remember. Unlike some runners who felt the pressures greatly, I think I always performed better inside an Olympic stadium.

—*Peter Snell, New Zealand*
track: 1 gold, 1960 Rome; 2 gold, 1964 Tokyo

*S*cared? I didn't even know where I was. It was the first time I'd been in front of a crowd that large and in the Olympic Games, competing against world record holders. I never thought I would even make it into the final round, much less have a very good throw on the first, which carried me through to a championship.

—*Al Oerter, United States*
discus: 4 gold, 1956 Melbourne, 1960 Rome,
1964 Tokyo, 1968 Mexico City
(about his first Olympics)

33

*E*veryone who goes to the Olympics dreams, expects or hopes to win, or at least perform well, and that, I think, is equal to winning a gold medal.

—*Ralph Doubell, Australia*
track: 1 gold, 1968 Mexico City

*E*very sportsman goes to a competition to win and become the champion. Everybody goes there for first place. Of course, in the end, I was the one who had the smile.

—*Naim Suleymanoglu, Turkey*
weightlifting: 3 gold, 1988 Seoul,
1992 Barcelona, 1996 Atlanta

*T*he way you psych someone out is not by using psychology. The way you psych someone out is by beating him ten meets in a row.

—Don Bragg, United States
pole vault: 1 gold, 1960 Rome

36

*M*y particular method of psyching out an opponent was of giving a real strong handshake before the race. I would squeeze his hand to give him the idea that this was what he was going to have to put up with—the strength of Mal Whitfield.

—*Mal Whitfield, United States*
track: 2 gold, 1 bronze, 1948 London;
1 gold, 1 silver, 1952 Helsinki

*I*n keen competition, the most important thing is to have a flexible game plan and to stay mentally alert to execute it.

—Murray Rose, Australia
swimming: 3 gold, 1956 Melbourne;
1 gold, 2 silver, 1960 Rome

FOCUS

*I*t is folly to forecast a tactic before a race. You must improvise your strategy according to your rival. You must empty your brain of everything around you and focus on your rival. Watch for and anticipate his every move and mistake. You must be flexible in your tactics, and have good reflexes and good judgment.

—Daniel Morelon, France
cycling: 1 bronze, 1964 Tokyo; 2 gold, 1968
Mexico City; 1 gold, 1972 Munich;
1 silver, 1976 Montreal

THE OLYMPIANS' GUIDE TO

*W*hen you're competing at the Olympics, you are really competing against yourself and with yourself. You're trying to get your body and mind to work at their optimal. If you let one of your competitors distract you from your focus on yourself, then they've won the battle and now have the edge on you. The very best competitors are the ones who can resist distractions, and can focus on the feedback their body and mind is giving them.

—*Mike Wenden, Australia*
swimming: 2 gold, 1 silver, 1 bronze,
1968 Mexico City

A lot of my competitors are afraid of me because my attitude on the track is that I'm out here to win races, period. Off the track we have a completely different relationship. But from the time I get out onto the track until I cross the finish line, I'm very focused on what I'm doing.

—*Michael Johnson, United States*
track: 1 gold, 1992 Barcelona;
2 gold, 1996 Atlanta

A lot of opponents underestimate my abilities because of my laid-back approach to the sport and the race itself. It doesn't take them but a couple of races to figure out that when it's time, I have the ability to hyper-focus on the task at hand.

—*Gary Hall Jr., United States*
swimming: 2 gold, 2 silver, 1996 Atlanta

*T*knew that if I could just make it to the Olympic team, I would have no problems. And that would make me a better athlete, because I wouldn't have anything to worry about except one thing, and that was competing. When you worry about just one thing, you're focused, and your mind and everything go toward one energy, one discipline, and everything works out.

—*Trent Dimas, United States*
gymnastics: 1 gold, 1992 Barcelona

*O*ne of the prime requisites of any good athlete is to be able to concentrate on the task at hand and tune out any noise or distraction that may exist around you. The moment your mind starts wandering, that's the time to start retiring.

—Tommy Kono, United States
weightlifting: 1 gold, 1952 Helsinki; 1 gold, 1956 Melbourne; 1 silver, 1960 Rome

*C*ompeting in track and field forms character. You know what you want to achieve. You are very concentrated. You work with the time you have, and that brings out an ability you can use for a lifetime.

—*Jurgen Hingsen, West Germany*
decathlon: 1 silver, 1984 Los Angeles

45

Topa, *topa*, *topa*: Look to ideals, but do not run away from reality. Make an endless wish, for if you concentrate and perfect yourself, you will break through the barriers.

—*Koji Gushiken, Japan*
gymnastics: 2 gold, 1 silver, 2 bronze,
1984 Los Angeles

DISCIPLINE

*I*t's 5:30, and it's snowy. It's Christmas Eve, but just think—nobody will be at the rink, and you can train for five hours straight. And it will all pay off someday.

—Carol Heiss, United States
figure skating: 1 silver, 1956 Cortina; 1 gold,
1960 Squaw Valley (recalling her mother's
encouragement, which motivated her
to become a world champion)

I don't mind that I've spent so much of my life in the ice rink, because there's so much that I learned there that I may not have learned elsewhere. I'm thinking in particular of self-discipline, ambition and will power.

—*Karin Kania, East Germany*
speed skating: 1 gold, 1980 Lake Placid; 2 gold,
2 silver, 1984 Sarajevo; 2 silver,
1 bronze, 1988 Calgary

*Y*es, the athletic experience transfers into everyday life. If you were disciplined enough to fight for something in the sports world, then you will be disciplined enough to be successful in the business world. Once you have been a winner, you believe you can be a winner in everything you do.

—*Louise Ritter, United States*
high jump: 1 gold, 1988 Seoul

49

My country did not send me 5,000 miles to start the race, they sent me 5,000 miles to finish the race.

—*John Stephen Akhwari, Tanzania*
marathon: 1968 Mexico City (finished bloodied
and bandaged in last place, one hour
after the winner)

I never dropped out of a race, mainly because I think that once you do, you've given yourself an option for the future.

—Dave Moorcroft, Great Britain
track: world record holder and favorite going into
the 5,000 meters, 1984 Los Angeles (suffered
recurrence of a preexisting injury during
the final, and finished last)

51

*T*hrust against pain...pain is the purifier.

—*Percy Cerutty*
coach of 1960 Olympic 1,500-meter gold
medalist, Herb Elliot of Australia

I knew when I descended from the rings that it would be the most painful moment in my life. I also knew that if my posture was not good, we would lose valuable points. I only had one choice: I must forget the pain.

—*Shun Fujimoto, Japan*
gymnastics: 1 gold, 1976 Montreal (continued in the
team event despite suffering a broken knee during
the floor exercise; Japan ended up winning
the gold by a mere .45 of a point)

53

*W*hen you really start to hurt at about 30 to 40 kilometers, then it comes down to who's got the mental capacity to push through all those pain barriers. And you have to do it alone. There's no one else out there. You're all by yourself.

—Bill Koch, United States
nordic skiing: 1 silver, 1976 Innsbruck

*E*very athlete has problems with pushing himself those small seconds or small centimeters further. You can do a lot with good training, but you can also do quite a lot with mental preparation.

—*Bjørn Dæhlie, Norway*
nordic skiing: 3 gold, 1 silver, 1992 Albertville;
2 gold, 2 silver, 1994 Lillehammer

*P*art of what appealed to me about sport was the mental preparation. When I swam against some of the great stars, I found that it wasn't just their strategy in the pool that was important, but the way they approached the race even before they entered the water.

—*Don Schollander, United States*
swimming: 4 gold, 1964 Tokyo; 1 gold,
1 silver, 1968 Mexico City

On purpose, my coach placed the shooting stand right in an anthill. When I shot from this stand on hot summer days, my legs were immediately covered with ants. This was very disturbing, especially when they reached my face.

—*Magnar Solberg, Norway*
biathlon: 1 gold, 1 silver, 1968 Grenoble;
1 gold, 1972 Sapporo (describing his training for
developing mental control; the biathlon is a mix of
cross-country skiing and target shooting)

*S*wimming taught me that sometimes sacrifice is necessary to accomplish something beneficial. It taught me you have to work hard. There were a lot of other things in my life that happened after the Olympics that were more important, but the Olympics helped me prepare for them.

—*Jeff Farrell, United States*
swimming: 2 gold, 1960 Rome (failed to qualify for
his favorite event, the 100-meter freestyle,
as he was recovering from appendicitis,
but went on to win 2 gold medals)

*T*here is an old expression that goes: If you cry during the week, you will laugh on Saturday. This means that if you work hard, practice and study during the week, then you will be successful when the test comes. Naturally, the reverse of this is also true, and should be avoided.

—*John Thomas, United States*
high jump: 1 bronze, 1960 Rome;
1 silver, 1964 Tokyo

*T*loved training and working hard. Every time I got in the water, I put my all into it. And I think that's the difference between someone making a team and getting a medal, and someone who almost made it.

—Debbie Meyer, United States
swimming: 3 gold, 1968 Mexico City

My theory has always been that if you want something, if you can see it, if you can visualize it and you are willing to pay the price of very hard work, then you can achieve it.

—*Herb McKenley, Jamaica*
track: 1 silver, 1948 London; 1 gold,
2 silver, 1952 Helsinki

CONFIDENCE

*I*t is very simple: To be a winner, you must have confidence in yourself, and to have confidence in yourself, you must work hard at your sport.

—*Sydney Maree, United States*
track: 1984 Los Angeles; 1988 Seoul (black South African track star and former 5,000-meter world record holder; he left his country to escape apartheid and compete in the Los Angeles and Seoul Games)

*W*hen you go to the Olympic Games, you have to believe in yourself. From my experience, the ones who believed in themselves the most were the ones who won.

—*Florence Griffith-Joyner, United States*
track: 1 silver, 1984 Los Angeles; 3 gold,
1 silver, 1988 Seoul

The farther you go up the ladder, the more confidence you have to get to the next rung.

—*Inger Miller, United States*
track: 1 gold, 1996 Atlanta

*T*f there's one thing I got out of track it was that if you could identify what your objective and goal were, things were much easier. I knew that I had to achieve certain things in practice and in preliminary races if I was going to win the Olympics or break the world's record in the half-mile. And when I achieved these, then I had the confidence that given the right conditions, I'd be able to do so in a race, too. And that did turn out to be true.

—*Tom Courtney, United States*
track: 2 gold, 1956 Melbourne

*O*vercoming adversity is a tremendous confidence booster. Now I feel that anything I really try for, I'll be able to achieve.

—*Silken Laumann, Canada*
rowing: 1 bronze, 1992 Barcelona; 1 silver, 1996
Atlanta (1991 world champion; she suffered a
severe leg injury in a boating accident just
a few months before the 1992 Olympics)

I endured a lot of pain because of my condition. Now when I train I think, "This is no worse than what I've experienced before. I can do just about anything now."

—*Greg Barton, United States*
kayak: 1 bronze, 1984 Los Angeles; 2 gold,
1988 Seoul; 1 bronze, 1992 Barcelona
(suffered painful surgery as a
child for his club feet)

THE OLYMPIANS' GUIDE TO

I never dream about losing. Positive thinking makes it happen sooner or later.

—Matt Ghaffari, United States
greco-roman wrestling: 1 silver, 1996 Atlanta

*N*aturally, you go into a race thinking you can win. You don't want to think you're going to get second, third or fourth, because if you think that way, you end up getting less than you set out to.

—Herman Frazier, United States
track: 1 gold, 1 bronze, 1976 Montreal

*S*omething inside of me kept saying, "There's still a chance, there's always still a chance." And I kept saying to myself, "I can win, I can win, I can win"—and the next thing I remember, I broke the tape.

—*Billy Mills, United States*
track: 1 gold, 1964 Tokyo (after his
10,000-meter upset victory)

It takes talent, discipline, a very strong work ethic and a love for your sport to be an Olympic champion. But that's only 50 percent of it. I wouldn't have become an Olympic champion without the other 50 percent that my coach, Bela Karoly, gave me. He made me believe the unbelievable, that I could be Olympic champion.

—Mary Lou Retton, United States
gymnastics: 1 gold, 2 silver, 2 bronze,
1984 Los Angeles

CHALLENGE

*D*octors and scientists said that breaking the four-minute mile was impossible, that one would die in the attempt. Thus, when I got up from the track after collapsing at the finish line, I figured I was dead.

—*Roger Bannister, Great Britain*
track: 1952 Helsinki (after becoming the first
man to break the 4-minute mile; he
finished fourth at Helsinki)

*P*eople say to me, "Call it a day," but I can't give up. I'm not saying I'm the world's best quarter miler, but I'm a quarter miler of some merit. And not knowing what I can do until I've exhausted all my chances and the time to prove it, I'm not going to stop...not for the moment.

—Derek Redmond, Great Britain
track: 1992 Barcelona (after missing his chance
to win a medal, due to a torn hamstring in
the semifinals; he hobbled to the finish
line with his father's support)

*M*any people have said, "You can't do that, Carl. It can't be done. A world-class athlete cannot do what you have done...endure so long." Well, I feel there are no limitations if you broaden your horizons. And if you don't succeed, you haven't failed, because you can't fail if you tried your hardest. So I hope I have inspired some people to do things they never thought they could do.

—Carl Lewis, United States
track and field: 4 gold, 1984 Los Angeles; 2 gold, 1 silver, 1988 Seoul; 2 gold, 1992 Barcelona; 1 gold, 1996 Atlanta

*T*he true measure of a great sportsman is his mental toughness after his physical and technical development has ended.

—*Pertti Karppinen, Finland*
rowing: 3 gold, 1976 Montreal,
1980 Moscow, 1984 Los Angeles

They all said, "You're too old and you haven't been in enough competition. You really should give it up." But then, that's my fighting nature. When someone says I can't do it, that's all I need. I took the challenge and, fortunately, was able to do it.

—*Sammy Lee, United States*
diving: 1 gold, 1 bronze, 1948 London; 1 gold, 1952 Helsinki (on winning his 2nd gold medal at age 32)

*T*he Seoul Olympics proved that older athletes can have fine performances. As long as one has motivation, is healthy and enjoys competition, success will follow, despite age.

—Kristin Otto, East Germany
swimming: 6 gold, 1988 Seoul (Otto was 22 at the Seoul Games, where 17- and 18-year-olds were considered to be at their peak)

I was told over and over again that I would never be successful, that I was not going to be competitive and the technique was simply not going to work. All I could do was shrug and say, "We'll just have to see."

—Dick Fosbury, United Sates
high jump: 1 gold, 1968 Mexico City (on reaction
to his revolutionary "Fosbury Flop" high-jump
technique, which not only won him the
gold, but also enabled him to set
an Olympic record)

*T*he '92 experience for me was unsurpassed in my swimming career. It was the realization of a lifelong dream. The fact that I was such an underdog and many people thought I didn't have a shot made the victory a bit sweeter. And also the fact that for a long time, I thought it was something that was never going to be accomplished.

—*Pablo Morales, United States*
swimming: 1 gold, 2 silver, 1984 Los Angeles;
2 gold, 1992 Barcelona

THE OLYMPIANS' GUIDE TO

$\mathcal{I}$can go fast even if I am little.

—*Janet Evans, United States*
swimming: 3 gold, 1988 Seoul; 1 gold, 1 silver,
1992 Barcelona (Evans was 5 feet 4 inches
and 95 pounds in 1988 when she
won three gold medals)

*T*used to fear the 1,000-meters race. So I began to write every day: I LOVE THE 1,000.... I LOVE THE 1,000. I would tape it up all over the house: on my bathroom mirror, on the refrigerator and in other strange places so I would see it all the time.

—Dan Jansen, United States
speed skating: 1 gold, 1994 Lillehammer
(after competing in four Olympics, Jansen
finally won the gold and set a world
record at Lillehammer)

*O*ne also has to overcome fear. Whenever I was able to overcome my fears, I had a feeling that I was really in control of myself. The fact is that a lot of competitors don't have this ability, and that's why they fail.

—*Vera Caslavska, Czechoslovakia*
gymnastics: 1 silver, 1960 Rome; 3 gold, 1 silver, 1964 Tokyo; 4 gold, 2 silver, 1968 Mexico City

*C*omplacency is a successful athlete's greatest psychological enemy. Once you start taking your victories for granted, someone will put an end to your winning streak. You must constantly find areas to improve.

—Steven Redgrave, Great Britain
rowing: 1 gold, 1984 Los Angeles; 1 gold,
1 bronze, 1988 Seoul; 1 gold, 1992
Barcelona; 1 gold, 1996 Atlanta

*W*hen one reaches the top, one feels that he has done all he set out to do. But that does not mean it is over. Now I must find another mountain to climb.

—*Vladimir Salnikov, USSR*
swimming: 3 gold, 1980 Moscow;
1 gold, 1988 Seoul

WINNING THE GAME OF LIFE

*T*hrough sport we learn judgment, teamwork, decision making and managing dimensions of time and space. Sport brings us to a higher level of thinking and exhibits our courage not only to win, but to participate and try.

—Anita DeFrantz, United States
rowing: 1 bronze, 1976 Montreal

*T*he thing to do in athletics if you are going to enjoy it is to test yourself. If you win, fine. If you lose, that gives you the incentive to keep trying. You have to train a bit harder, and you have to come back again and again. That is the joy.

—*Ron Clarke, Australia*
track: 1 bronze, 1964 Tokyo (holder of 21 world records, but only won one medal at the Olympics)

RESILIENCE

*W*hen I lost, I would think, well, I just have to work harder and win the next race, that's all. I didn't like to lose, but I thought, well, I'll forget about this race and think about the next one.

—*Gaetan Boucher, Canada*
speed skating: I silver, 1980 Lake Placid;
2 gold, 1 bronze, 1984 Sarajevo

*A*thletes shouldn't be too disappointed when they lose a race. They should take it as a lesson and look forward to the next one.

—*Mike Boit, Kenya*
track: 1 bronze, 1972 Munich

osing gives you a chance to start again.

—Wolfgang Hoppe, Germany
bobsled: 2 gold, 1984 Sarajevo; 2 silver, 1988
Calgary; 1 silver, 1992 Albertville; 1
bronze, 1994 Lillehammer

think failure is one of the great motivators. After my narrow loss in the 1948 trials, I knew how really good I could be. It was the defeat that focused all my concentration on my training and my goals.

—*Pat McCormick, United States*
diving: 2 gold, 1948 London; 2 gold, 1952 Helsinki

*T*t's easy to be a champion. You just go with the flow. But to be a second- and third-place finisher, you learn more about yourself, what you think about yourself. And how to pull yourself up by the proverbial bootstraps.

—*Ralph Boston, United States*
long jump: 1 gold, 1960 Rome; 1 silver, 1964
Tokyo; 1 bronze, 1968 Mexico City

*G*oing into the final, I read one of the press clippings that predicted I would freeze because of my failure to make the finals at the Moscow Games. I went in there trying to counter this negativism with lots of positive thinking, but I was still frightened to death. So before we went onto the field, I located the world record holder and the best thrower on my team, and plunked myself right down between the two of them. I guess it worked.

—*Tessa Sanderson, Great Britain*
javelin: 1 gold, 1984 Los Angeles

T was not only proud of what he did in the pool, but I was proud of the way he handled himself out of the pool. The measure of a true champion is not how they win. It's how they handle defeat.

—Gary Hall Sr., United States
swimming: 1 silver, 1968 Mexico City; 1 silver, 1972
Munich; 1 bronze, 1976 Montreal (about his son,
Gary Hall Jr., who won 2 golds in relays,
but finished 2nd to Russia's Alexander
Popov in the 50- and 100-meter
freestyle at the Atlanta Games)

*E*verything you pursue you won't always attain. That's probably the most important lesson I learned from missing that race. There are times in life when you may not get the raise you want, the job you want. You have to learn to live with your defeats. And athletics are valuable, because they're all about winning and losing. Before you can actually be a good winner, you have to know how to lose.

—*Eddie Hart, United States*
track: 1 gold, 1972 Munich (missed his 100-meter
heat because of a scheduling mixup, losing
his chance for an individual gold medal)

*U*ntil you learn to lose, you can't win.

Toni Sailer, Austria
alpine skiing: 3 gold, 1956 Cortina

*T*here was a great deal of anxiety and pressure on me before the match. Though I fought hard, Geesink dominated. It was still a great experience for me, and whenever I am faced with difficulties in my work life, I think back to those days of training, and my problems seem so insignificant in comparison that I am able to go on.

—Akio Kaminaga, Japan

judo: 1 silver, 1964 Tokyo (suffered an embarrassing upset loss to Anton Geesink of the Netherlands in Tokyo, where judo was introduced to the Games)

I want to inspire kids in some way and let them know that the road will not always be easy. In fact, it will be hard at times, but you're going to have to take a deep breath...and don't look back.

—*Calvin Smith, United States*
track: 1 gold, 1984 Los Angeles;
1 bronze, 1988 Seoul

97

I wouldn't ask them to reverse their decision. I don't live in the past. I live in the present and prepare for the future.

—*Ralph Metcalf, United States*
track: 1 silver, 1 bronze, 1932 Los Angeles; 1 gold, 1 silver, 1936 Berlin (in two controversial decisions, finished 2nd to Eddie Tolan in the 100 and 200 meters in 1932; also finished 2nd to Jesse Owens in the 100 in 1936; he was later elected to the House of Representatives from the State of Illinois)

*T*he funny thing about sports is that one day you are on top, and the next day you're on the bottom. You can never be sure about the future.

—*Oksana Baiul, Ukraine*
figure skating: 1 gold, 1994 Lillehammer

THE OLYMPIANS' GUIDE TO

*J*udo means "the gentle way"... yielding is strength...gentle turns away sturdy... bend like bamboo, and then strike back.

—*the philosophy instilled in Judo players*

PASSION

I have a long career because I'm persistent. But I also have passion. I love sports. I love cycling, and I love to try to improve myself. I set a goal and do everything possible to reach it.

—Jeannie Longo Ciprelli, France
cycling: 1 silver, 1992 Barcelona; 1 gold, 1996 Atlanta (won the gold at age 38)

I never run with my watch when I run a race. I have to run how I feel. If I feel good, I run fast. If I don't feel that good, I don't run fast. I don't run for records. I run trying to win.

—*Grete Waitz, Norway*
marathon: 1 silver, 1984 Los Angeles

I run for my country, my family and mostly I guess for myself, because I enjoy track. Track has made me feel good, and when you feel good within yourself, then a lot revolves around that. You have a happier life.

—*Valerie Brisco, United States*
track: 3 gold, 1984 Los Angeles;
1 silver, 1988 Seoul

I am the kind of sportsman who doesn't go for the gold, doesn't go for the silver, I simply go for it! And if I win, that is great, but if I don't, that is fine, too. The most important thing is to enjoy it, to love your sport, and then you can be happy with any result.

—*Anton Geesink, The Netherlands*
judo: 1 gold, 1964 Tokyo

*M*y enjoyment obviously comes from winning, but more than anything else it comes from performing well. I think that, having performed well, I wouldn't mind coming in second or third. Because at the end of the day, I'm the only one I really have to please.

—*Daley Thompson, Great Britain*
decathlon: 1 gold, 1980 Moscow;
1 gold, 1984 Los Angeles

*T*here's an enjoyment in doing something well. Whatever it is, if you can fulfill your potential in a particular area, that gives you a great deal of satisfaction.

—*Ric Charlesworth, Australia*
field hockey: 1 silver, 1976 Montreal

*P*eople often ask me, "What's your secret?" My only secret is that I really want to do it.

—*Maurilio De Zolt, Italy*
nordic skiing: 1 silver, 1988 Calgary; 1 silver, 1992
Albertville; 1 gold, 1994 Lillehammer
(won the gold at age 43)

107

I took some time off and said, "I'm going to love my sport again. I'm going to do it for me and no one else." It taught me how to handle my life now. If I was able to get through something like that, I can get through anything. It's put a real positive mark on my attitude toward life.

—*Elizabeth Manley, Canada*
figure skating: 1 silver, 1988 Calgary

*Y*ou've got to have dreams and hopes, and you can't let anybody take them away from you. I remember when I was 13, my first coach saying, "You're too small. You're 5 feet 2 inches. You barely weigh 100 pounds. You can't possibly hope to do what you want to do." And I went and did it.

—*Donna de Varona, United States*
swimming: 2 gold, 1964 Tokyo

109

*W*hen I was five, I desperately wanted a pair of ice skates for Christmas. Among the presents under the tree...I knew which package held the skates because the blade had broken through the wrapping, and I could see the toe sticking out. It was the only present I remember getting through my whole childhood.

—*Dick Button, United States*
figure skating: 1 gold, 1948 St. Moritz;
1 gold, 1952 Oslo

PERFORMANCE

*I*t takes a lot of experience, a lot of training and a lot of previous competitions to get ready for the big races. Because once the gun goes off, there isn't a lot of thinking, just instinct.

—Bonnie Blair, United States
speed skating: 1 gold, 1 bronze, 1988 Calgary;
2 gold, 1992 Albertville; 2 gold,
1994 Lillehammer

I don't think anybody can feel that the Olympic final is theirs until they cross the finish line. That has been proven before when people have eased up, and on the last few inches, someone's gone past them. In the Olympic final I was told to drive right through the line, and that's exactly what I did.

—*Steve Ovett, Great Britain*
track: 1 gold, 1 bronze, Moscow 1980
(on leading during the final stretch
of his gold medal race)

112

*F*eet, don't fail me now.

—many athletes during their final

moments to victory

*M*y strategy was to start the race fast, finish the race fast and win the race.

—*Armin Hary, West Germany*
track: 2 gold, 1960 Rome

*E*ven after 104 races, this particular race is a one-shot deal. You only get one chance, and this one is for all the marbles. Even though you go in as well-prepared as you can be, there are so many unknown variables you never even consider that can be your demise.

—Edwin Moses, United States
track: 1 gold, 1976 Montreal; 1 gold, 1984
Los Angeles; 1 bronze, 1988 Seoul

THE OLYMPIANS' GUIDE TO

It was a lifetime of training for just 10 seconds.

—Jesse Owens, United States
track and field: 4 gold, 1936 Berlin
(after winning the 100 meters)

*J*esse Owens said the 100 meters was a lifetime of training for just 10 seconds. I say the 110 hurdles is 13 seconds and 10 hurdles of sheer effort and concentration.

—*Rod Milburn, United States*
track: 1 gold, 1976 Montreal

*I*t's not necessarily the fastest man who's going to win. It's the one who makes the least mistakes.

—*Peter Norman, Australia*
track: 1 silver, 1968 Mexico City

118

The easiest and most efficient way to win a race is to win by a small margin. Don't try any heroics.

—*Matthew Pinsent, Great Britain*
rowing: 1 gold, 1992 Barcelona;
1 gold, 1996 Atlanta

In dressage, as in life, you must achieve the perfect harmony. If you push too much, you destroy the harmony; if you don't push, nothing happens.

—*Reiner Klimke, West Germany*
equestrian/dressage: 6 gold, 2 bronze, 1964–1988

The relationship between a rider and his horse must be one of perfect harmony. It is just like Fred Astaire and Ginger Rogers, absolutely the same.

—*Hans Winkler, West Germany*
equestrian: 2 gold, 1956 Melbourne; 1 gold, 1960
Rome; 1 gold, 1964 Tokyo; 1 gold, 1972
Munich; 1 silver, 1976 Montreal

*T*o be a good figure skater you need the balance of a tightrope walker, the nerves of a golfer, the strength of a football player, the agility of a gymnast and the grace of a ballet dancer. All of that.

—*Tenley Albright, United States*
figure skating: 1 silver, 1952 Oslo;
1 gold, 1956 Cortina

In 1973 after the Munich games, I was brought to the White House to meet President Richard Nixon. He said that my performances in Munich did more to reduce the political tensions between our two countries than the embassies were able to do in five years.

—Olga Korbut, USSR
gymnastics: 3 gold, 1 silver, 1972 Munich;
1 gold, 1 silver, 1976 Montreal

ACHIEVEMENT

I believe that a person's true happiness comes from being able to look back in their past and feel they worked hard to achieve something and, in fact, achieved it.

—Hirofumi Daimatsu

coach of the Japanese women's gold-medal winning volleyball team in the 1964 Tokyo Games (known for his ruthless training methods)

*W*hen you achieve great things, people expect greatness. But no matter what others expect, the desire to succeed must come from yourself.

—Christa Rothenburger-Luding,
East Germany
speed skating/cycling: 1 gold, 1984 Sarajevo; 1
gold, 1 silver, 1988 Calgary; 1 silver, 1988
Seoul; 1 bronze, 1992 Albertville

I am a person who is free to make my own choices, but I wouldn't consider myself independent. During my career I have depended on the support of my family, coaches and friends for much of the success I have attained.

—*Manuela Di Centa, Italy*
cross-country skiing: 2 gold, 2 silver,
1 bronze, 1994 Lillehammer

*W*inning a medal involves the support of many people. It's not just the athlete and the coach. It's also the guy who cleans the pool and the lady who cleans the showers. Everyone does their best so that we can win a medal. I consider myself at the tip of a gigantic pyramid of supporters who pushed me to win that medal.

—*Filipe Munoz, Mexico*
swimming: 1 gold, 1968 Mexico City

*T*he athlete becomes a champion when he realizes a humbleness that joins his physical and psychological selves.

—*Alberto Cova, Italy*
track: 1 gold, 1984 Los Angeles

After that first small success, you realize you have potential, then you want to see how far you can reach.

—*Lasse Viren, Finland*
track: 2 gold, 1972 Munich; 2
gold, 1976 Montreal

129

I was the first Kenyan to beat the 4-minute mile, the first to break the Olympic record, the first to break the world record, but this was an achievement only for me. I wanted to do something for my country. This life we have is short, so let us leave a mark for people to remember.

—*Kip Keino, Kenya*
track: 1 gold, 1 silver, 1968 Mexico City; 1 gold, 1
silver, 1972 Munich (on why he adopted and
educated 69 orphan Kenyan children)

*O*ne should take on as many respon-
sibilities as possible. For if you do,
there are more chances you will achieve
great things.

—*Alexander Karelin, Russia*
greco-roman wrestling: 3 gold, 1988 Seoul,
1992 Barcelona, 1996 Atlanta

131

*T*think the objective in all athletics should be to develop the characteristics that make an individual not only a winner in sports, but a winner in whatever becomes one's life work and in one's day-to-day living.

—*Glenn Cunningham, United States*

track: 1 silver, 1936 Berlin

*G*oing into each competition my goal was never to win the gold, the silver or the bronze medal. My goal—what I would tell myself—was, do your event in the best possible way you can, and if you do, you will have a chance to win.

—*Larysa Latynina, USSR*

gymnastics: 4 gold, 1 silver, 1 bronze, 1956
Melbourne; 3 gold, 2 silver, 1 bronze,
1960 Rome; 2 gold, 2 silver,
2 bronze, 1964 Tokyo

*Y*ou need goals in life because it's the only way you can get through it. Everybody has a goal. Washing dishes is a goal, too.

—*Yvonne van Gennip, The Netherlands*
speed skating: 3 gold, 1988 Calgary

*P*art of the joy of being a champion or of trying to achieve a number-one spot is all that goes into getting there.

—*Mark Spitz, United States*
swimming: 2 gold, 1 silver, 1 bronze, 1968
Mexico City; 7 gold, 1972 Munich

When I was sick was the year I learned the most of my whole career. I now know how hard it is to lose. If you always win, everything is so easy and you don't think about why it's been good. When you lose and then win again, you feel it more deeply.

—*Gunde Svan, Sweden*
nordic skiing: 2 gold, 1 silver, 1 bronze,
1984 Sarajevo; 2 gold, 1988 Calgary

*W*hen I came to the Olympics, I thought I was only going to win gold medals. But it's not so easy. When I won, I understood what it cost to win. It's always a hard struggle.

—*Vladimir Smirnov, Kazakhstan*
nordic skiing: 2 silver, 1 bronze, 1988 Calgary;
1 gold, 2 silver, 1994 Lillehammer

*L*ife is not simply holding a good hand,
life is playing a poor hand well.

—*popular Danish saying*
(used to describe Lis Hartel's silver medal victories in
dressage at the 1952 Helsinki and 1956 Melbourne
Olympics; Hartel was partially paralyzed
after contracting polio in 1944)

138

I'm not the tallest kid in the world. I'm not the fastest kid in the world. I found a sport I could do well in and achieve what other great athletes have. There are sports out there for everyone.

—*Justin Huish, United States*
archery: 2 gold, 1996 Atlanta

*W*hen I was young I had a speech impediment. It was frustrating because I would stand in front of the class and make all these mistakes, and they would ridicule me. So I directed my energy to what I could do physically. I showed people that I could dance, do gymnastics—and I could dive.

—*Greg Louganis, United States*
diving: 2 gold, 1984 Los Angeles;
2 gold, 1988 Seoul

RECOGNITION

*I*t was a tremendous relief that we had done the job we were sent there to do. And a real thrill that for once, probably the only time in my life, I was the best in the world.

—*David Wight, United States*
rowing: 1 gold, 1956 Melbourne

*E*very athlete remembers the days of difficult training and suffering. At the same time, during the brief moment she wins, she forgets all that suffering and thinks only of the fact that she is the champion, that the whole world respects and applauds her.

—*Ghada Shouaa, Syria*
heptathlon: 1 gold, 1996 Atlanta

*T*he proudest moment for me was not crossing the finish line, not having the gold medal put around my neck, but when they played the national anthem and I knew that I was responsible for it happening...and that nearly 12 million people back in Australia were thrilled out of their brains that I had won.

—*Herb Elliot, Australia*
track: 1 gold, 1960 Rome

143

I was slightly outside my body, looking on, because it was a very emotional moment when the flag went up and the national anthem was played. And you just can't really believe that this ordinary person has suddenly done something extraordinary.

—*Ann Packer, Great Britain*
track: 1 gold, 1 silver, 1964 Tokyo

A lot of what keeps you training is the idea that you're going to make the Olympic team and then maybe be up there on the winner's platform. And then you get up there, and there's this realization that you're actually there. That's overwhelming in a way because there's always, at least in me, a little bit of self-doubt. But suddenly, there wasn't any reason to be doubtful.

—*Frank Shorter, United States*
marathon: 1 gold medal, 1972 Munich;
1 silver, 1976 Montreal

*R*eceiving the medal, hearing the national anthem...at the time I did not think about anything. The reaction came the following day when I opened the papers and they had written in large print DA SILVA OLYMPIC CHAMPION. DA SILVA WORLD RECORD HOLDER. It was at that moment I understood I had really won the event.

Adhemar da Silva, Brazil
triple jump: 1 gold, 1952 Helsinki;
1 gold, 1956 Melbourne

*I*f you're going to give someone flow-ers, make sure they're around to smell them.

—*John Davis, United States*
weightlifting: 1 gold, 1948 London;
1 gold, 1952 Helsinki

*B*e polite, be modest, be honest, be friendly, sign autographs, be available. It is the most important thing for a champion to be a good human being.

—*Alberto Juantorena, Cuba*

track: 2 gold, 1976 Montreal

*D*ear Pappy, thanks for waiting for me to get born. I'm coming home with the gold medal you should have won in 1924.

—*Frank Havens, United States*
canoeing: 1 silver, 1948 London; 1 gold, 1952
Helsinki (recognizing his father, Bill Haven's,
sacrifice in giving up the opportunity to
compete at the 1924 Olympics to
stay by his pregnant wife's side)

THE OLYMPIANS' GUIDE TO

AFFIRMATION

*N*o matter what sort of pain you go through, it's worth it because it's going to give you a lifetime of memories.

—*Henry Marsh, United States*
steeplechase: 1984 Los Angeles (after collapsing
in exhaustion at the finish line and missing
the bronze medal by mere inches)

*I*f that's the biggest disappointment in my life, then I've had a pretty good life. I enjoy my sport, but it's not everything in life. Sports are to have fun.

Grant Davies, Australia

kayak: 1 silver, 1988 Seoul (finished the race in a near-dead heat; the scoreboard flashed Davies' name as the winner, but a few minutes later, Greg Barton of the United States was declared the winner of the gold)

*W*hen an athlete competes with an injury, you anticipate a drop. Like a roller coaster going up the tracks, you know the drop on the other side is going to be devastating, frustrating, painful or scary. But if you enjoy the ride—you enjoy giving your best despite adversity—you'll get pleasure on the ups and the downs.

—*Bob Kersee*
coach and husband of Jackie Joyner-Kersee,
three-time Olympic champion

To take the long jump down to the sixth attempt and come away with the bronze medal was, to me, more gratifying than any gold medal I won, because it tested my character, my strength...what I believe athletics is all about.

—Jackie Joyner-Kersee, United States
track and field: 1 silver, 1984 Los Angeles; 2 gold, 1988 Seoul; 1 gold, 1 bronze, 1992 Barcelona; 1 bronze, 1996 Atlanta

I can hold my head up high. I really tried, I tried honestly, I tried fairly... but it wasn't to be at the Olympic Games. I went to the Olympics because that's what it's all about—making the effort, being a true sportsman. Whatever the results, you accept them.

—Eamonn Coghlan, Ireland
track: 1976 Montreal, 1980 Moscow, 1988 Seoul
(former indoor world record holder in the mile,
after finishing 4th in Montreal and Moscow,
and then last in the semifinals in Seoul)

154

*A*t the time I lost, I was quite disappointed with myself. But now, looking back, I value the experience of knowing how a second-place finisher feels.

—*Sawao Kato, Japan*
gymnastics: 3 gold, 1 bronze, 1968 Mexico City;
3 gold, 2 silver, 1972 Munich; 2 gold,
1 silver, 1976 Montreal

THE OLYMPIANS' GUIDE TO

*F*ourth place in a world of four billion people isn't so bad.

—*Lennox Miller, Jamaica*
track: 1 silver, 1968 Mexico City; 1 bronze, 1972
Munich (to his daughter, Inger, after she
barely missed winning a medal in the
200 meters at the Atlanta Games)

I was born, bred and reared in the Mississippi Delta cotton fields. Athletics was my flight to freedom, my escape. I discovered that through athletics you could see the world. I could get an education. I am who I am because of my participation in sport and my Olympic experience. I did not win a gold medal in athletics, but I did win the gold medal of life.

—Willye White, United States
track: 1 silver, 1956 Melbourne;
1 silver, 1964 Tokyo

THE OLYMPIANS' GUIDE TO

The important thing at the Olympic Games is not winning, but taking part. The essential thing is not conquering, but fighting well.

—*Baron Pierre de Coubertin*
founder of the modern Olympic Games

INDEX